Are the Students Learning?

Igniting student learning while improving a student-centered class.

(VOLUME 1)

It is a honor to present my first book signed to Debbie.

from. Dr. Evans Akpo (Author)

Evans Igho Akpo

ISBN 978-1-0980-8947-4 (paperback)
ISBN 978-1-0980-8948-1 (digital)

Copyright © 2021 by Evans Igho Akpo

All rights reserved. No part of this publication may be reproduced, distributed, or transmitted in any form or by any means, including photocopying, recording, or other electronic or mechanical methods without the prior written permission of the publisher. For permission requests, solicit the publisher via the address below.

Christian Faith Publishing, Inc.
832 Park Avenue
Meadville, PA 16335
www.christianfaithpublishing.com

Printed in the United States of America

I dedicate this work to Dr. Margaretha E. Bischoff on her retirement from South Texas College in McAllen, Texas. She was the best Dean in an academic institution anyone can ever imagine working with.

To the memory of Bill Green on his transition, he was the Assistant Chair of the Political Science Department of South Texas College. He wrote my doctoral recommendation letters and provided wonderful support, but did not live to see the effort he invested in.

To my wife for her support during the process of writing this book, and the commitment she has shown our family and my demanding academic work. I am beyond proud of her unexplainable patience.

PREFACE

In its fundamental sense, community colleges and other educational institutions understand that the key to successfully delivering on their commitment to educate and prepare future generations of students fall squarely on the shoulders of the person standing at the front of every classroom. The teacher, lecturer, or professor has always been the most critical part of any education system. The question is not if they are teaching, because they are doing a great job teaching. The question—based on the statistics of students who graduate—is whether the students are learning.

The purpose of this book is *not* to explain all the reasons students are not learning, nor is it to examine all the theories of learning. It is not going to address all the correlations of learning, which may include gender, disability, and sociocultural and systemic barriers in all education. Other books have produced excellent work on the aspect of learning. For example, Jean Lave and Etienne Wenger's work has provided an excellent explanation of learning within social relationships.

While Lave and Wenger's work concludes that all beginning learning takes place in a "situated learning" environment which has a relationship with language, context, and culture, the author provides a synopsis of his work based on experiences in South Texas in the United States with a limited student population, predominantly Latino. While the solution may apply to most students, this book is not indicative of all community colleges or institutions around the world because sociocultural, political, religion, and school policies may differ. However, the principle of whether students are learning may share some common vital characteristics as there is no precise one-size-fits-all technique. The writer hopes this book provides some solutions to student learning and helps teachers, policymakers, and educators create a system that would support student learning. The ultimate purpose is to help educators create a student-centered class that helps students succeed.

The theoretical framework for this book is centered on one condition of Tinto's (2012) persistence theory which is learning.

The author is aware that this book is not designed to provide all the solutions. Most importantly, this book is focused mainly on three aspects of students learning. The author acknowledges the criticism that it is not peer-reviewed, hence it may be viewed from a different perspective. Nevertheless, the insight of the practices has not been discounted because of the rich knowledge and experience of the valuable contributors.

ACKNOWLEDGMENTS

Many people contributed to this work, to which I am most grateful. I want to acknowledge the work of Cheryl E. Joseph for providing research materials with her valuable time. To Carmella R. Blackshear and Kimberly Joyner, the Advising Manager of Houston Community College, College of Health for their support and professional exposure to student advising.

My profound gratitude to the Dean of Student Success, Dr. Patricia Ugwu for her unspeakable assistance and support in ensuring I succeed and earn my doctorate. My regards to Mrs. Kumudu.

This work would be incomplete without the input of Dr. Robert Ballinger and Ms. Mary Rios of South Texas College in McAllen, Texas, for their generous support in several ways.

My ceaseless respect to my community college mentor, Dr. Elizabeth Huffman, and Professor Martin Morales of Cosumnes College, Sacramento, California. for their continuous contribution and immense support.

My proud appreciation to Dr. Diane Reed, Dr. Kristie Celing and Dr. James Bevers for their support during my doctoral academic program.

Thanks to Ms. Patti Dali for the edition of the manuscript. Her commitment to the success of this work is encouraging.

Thank you, Dr. Edythe Weeks for always making complex concepts easy in all your analysis.

CONTENTS

Learning Process 19
Learning from the Students Perspective 22
How Teachers Can Ignite Learning 26
Why Students Do Not Learn 33
References 49

Are the Students Learning?

Igniting student learning while improving a student-centered class.

(VOLUME 1)

Are the Students Learning?
Igniting Student Learning While
Improving a Student-centered Class.
(Volume 1)

An interview in 2017 with Dr. Margaretha E. Bischoff, Dean for Liberal Arts & Social Sciences at South Texas College in McAllen, Texas, prompted the writing of this book, and she asked a keen question. The few minutes of the interview with her for a full-time position changed my perspective on learning. It was as if a new trajectory of my career emerged after my conversation with her.

Her question was, "I wonder if the students are learning, are the students learning?" With her calm, friendly, and characteristic Dutch accent, patiently waiting for an answer, she paused. Before that moment, I thought about learning from a passive sense as opposed to an active and intentional position. At the interview, I was explaining how I was teaching and the strategies I was employing to get my right foot in the door. From a professional perspective, it seems she understands that teaching on the part of the teacher doesn't necessarily translate into learning on the part of students.

In most interviews, applicants present an explanation of their teaching strategies, coupled with their teaching philosophies. As important as it seems, it often suggests the interviewee is making every effort to hone their best skills to acquire the position. After all, teachers teach. In my case with Dr. Bischoff, an experienced dean and a former classroom lecturer, she was passionate and curious about whether students are learning.

Learning would mean "understanding what is being taught." You could tell she was passionate about student learning from the silence that interjected our conversation. At South Texas College, the vision is to be a global model in educational innovation, catalyzing to drive regional prosperity, economic development, and the social mobility of students. During the interview, I observed that Dr. Bischoff's interest in student learning aligns with the school mission of providing higher educational opportunities through excellence in teaching and learning, workforce development, cultural enrichment, community service, and regional and global collaborations. Her words seem to focus on learning.

Our conversation led me to think about my experience with Professor Tom Villis in British

American College, London, several years ago. In the professor's class for a whole semester, I did not learn most things he was teaching. Although he was one of the best teachers in the school, there was disconnection between teaching and learning. Tom Villis, a graduate of Cambridge University, was arguably one of the best professors on campus. His work clearly highlights his excellence in teaching, which is evident from all his students' performance. However, in one of his classes, I learned so much and in the other class I never learned. While I was the common denominator, I started thinking about what a change of strategy would have impacted my ability to learn. With these thoughts, Dr. Bischoff's question kept coming to mind.

LEARNING PROCESS

> Don't limit a child to your own learning,
> for he/she was born in another time.
> (Rabindranath Tagore)

Most students who set out to earn degrees in community colleges never complete their programs. According to Baker (2016), interventions that simplify the complex organizational structures of the schools are promising. However, beyond the interventions that seek to prevent dropouts, there are several reasons enrollment has not translated into graduation. Researchers have worked endlessly in providing solutions for the reasons students leave institutions of learning without completion. Considering the negative impact incomplete studies have on the economy, it is essential to note that society pays when completion rates are low. Taxpayers, who provide the majority of the funding are at a disadvantage for subsidizing the amenities of those students who never complete college use when they enroll. Studies show that those who take on student loans and do not complete degrees are much more likely to default on their student loans than students who graduate (Hillman, 2014).

In a study conducted by Baker (2016), the researcher provided rigorous evidence of the efforts of the effects of the structure transfer program; most researchers have commended the great work, yet concluded it is an incomplete analysis without the core subject of whether or not the students are learning. It is hard in the social sciences to say that any one factor is the sole cause of any phenomenon or policy outcome. For example, one cannot say learning is the only reason students fail to graduate. Learning has been a central topic in psychological research virtually since the conception of psychology as an independent science (Ebbinghaus, 1885, 1962; Thorndike, 1911). However, besides learning, there must be other factors that contribute to such failures to graduate.

Learning is addressed in virtually all areas of psychology. It is worth noting that researchers are rarely explicit about what they mean by the term "learning." Existing literature about learning does not always contain a definition of its subject matter (Bouton, 2007; Schwartz, Wasserman, & Robbins, 2002). What remains consistent is that there is no general agreement about the definition of learning. To some extent, the lack of consensus about the definition of learning is not surprising because it is difficult to define concepts adequately, especially concepts that are as broad and abstract as the concept of learning. With the existing challenges of defining learning, it may be unwise to conclude that definitional issues be ignored. Researchers likely carry with them some ideas of what learning is.

Without an inherent sense of what learning is, there would be no reason for devoting time and energy to studying it, in that process, explicitly addressing definitional issues can help avoid misunderstandings and facilitate communication among learning researchers.

Given the narrative above, this book will address learning from the perspective of its contribution to students staying in college without discounting other components.

LEARNING FROM THE STUDENTS PERSPECTIVE

The notion of students experiencing learning before formal education stems from the sociocultural theory. Thus, learning from a student perspective took place before students came into any formal institutions. According to sociocultural theory, the interaction between student culture and the current formal education in which they are exposed to have an impact on learning. Students can only know or understand the world through the mental framework that transforms, organizes, and interprets their perceptions before they come into formal education. Knowledge, according to Fosnot (1989), consists of past constructions because as we interact with our environment and try to make sense of our experiences, we can reflect and learn. Meaningful learning occurs through reflection and resolutions.

While teaching may be taking place in class, there may be a disconnection between teaching and learning. According to McGuire (2015), focusing almost exclusively on teaching and ignoring how teachers can help students in the learning process creates an imbalance in the equation. Based on the researcher's experience, even if we have the best teachers on the planet, students need learning skills to succeed before they can have some improvements. The researcher stresses that only when students are actively engaged in the learning process will they be able to learn in any circumstance.

Active learning, from a student perspective, can only be said to occur when teachers are able to make the connection. As Brian Bedford, former Dean of Business at Cosumnes River College puts it, "teaching is about making the connection with students. Without the needed connection, teaching cannot take place." It is the connection that creates a student's ability to learn, although numerous arguments exist that there is minimal teaching taking place in schools.

According to the work of Gallimore and Tharp (1990), teachers, administrators, and professors engage in the process of assigning and assessing. The daily activity of what teachers define as teaching is primarily concerned with assigning tasks, activities, monitoring those activities, and ensuring students complete the tasks, then they grade those activities. This method of teaching is what critics point out as the contrast with the work of Vygotsky's (1962) movement, which is more collaborative as opposed to isolated and individualized activities. With the process of teaching being an individual performance, it defeats the social interaction that take place in learning. Learning happens when a specific type of social interaction occurs that must be designed by teachers to assist students in creating meaning.

The instructional strategy of recitation and memorization of facts creates limited knowledge. Most teaching that defeats learning may be well-meaning, yet teachers engage in the process of teaching by providing knowledge to students and requesting memorization and recitation of facts, and then are graded for it. This process of memorization and recitation presented by students has not provided students the opportunity to construct meaning from comprehensive input. While school administrators, teachers, educational policymakers, and school stakeholders may require the students respond in specific ways rather than engaging them with the materials and ideas, it makes the process of learning difficult.

HOW TEACHERS CAN IGNITE LEARNING

> "Cause to learn." Teachers should accept the responsibility of causing students to learn.
> (Dr. Bruce Wilkinson)

The accurate pivotal contact in the educational system has been and always will be the teachers. According to Wilkinson (2010), a teacher can control the style, settings, and speaker of the class, which influences how students learn. While a teacher cannot force learning, the way in which a teacher controls the parameters control how students were learning. According to Hufstedler (1979) the former U.S. Secretary of Education, "the secret of being a successful teacher is to accept in a very personal way the responsibility for each student's success or failure.

Those teachers who do take personal responsibility for their students' success and failure tend to produce higher-achieving students." [Video] Teachers should judge their success by the success of their students. A teacher plays a greater role beyond what most students and institutions can imagine, and their role and job description have kept increasing over the years. While such an increased role doesn't often translate to increased pay commensurate with the current U.S. inflation rate, most teachers sacrifice so much to bring out the best in their students.

McGuire (2015) in *Teach students: How to Learn* stated the struggles some faculty members may face and lament over, arguing that the students' lack of academic preparation is the primary reason that students are not successful. In challenging that assumption, McGuire highlights how quickly unprepared students gained lost grounds with good learning strategies from teachers. Good learning strategies presented for teachers show that with established high expectations and clearly defined student success, most students are inclined to learn. Clear expectations, according to Gabriel's *Teaching Unprepared Students* (2008), is especially essential for students who are not very prepared for classroom or campus culture.

Teachers are essential to the academic institution because of the great job they do in advancing learning processes. As Boyer (1997) stated at the Carnegie Foundation for the Advancement of Teaching highlights, "all the conversation about excellence in teaching are superficial unless we acknowledge that good teaching is in the heart of a good school (para. 2)."

The educational institution has expanded on the idea that the first quality of excellent teaching is the very human characteristic of love and concern for others. It is the intention of the teacher to take active steps to be involved in the student learning space. Without the teacher's determination to demand more of the students (to encourage them to work hard and employ instructional strategies that provide a supportive, caring, and learning environment directed towards student-centeredness), most students will not learn. However, the frustration for most teachers, especially well-meaning teachers, is not that they do not understand that teaching and learning should be a pleasurable experience, nor do they not have teaching behavior that promotes pleasant, positive experience in the classroom. Most teachers know that teaching is one of the keys to student learning. The fact is that most schools are doing the best they can as it relates to teachers. Teachers are pivotal to the educational environment. Admittedly, teaching is a complex activity; hence, it is out of place for it to be designed from a myopic perspective and assign a simple cause and effect relationship to either the successful or unsuccessful outcomes.

Based on the sufficient work of teachers, it is time for educators to take a breath and examine what happens in the classroom and the variables that appear to have impacted student learning. Studies show that teachers' expectations of students do indeed correlate with the level of students' performance. Teachers impact more by their character and their commitment than by their communication. Furthermore, because of that, the teacher exists to serve the students.

O'Dowd (2015) articulated this idea more clearly when he stated that my job is not so much to teach as it is to help students learn. You can teach to a wall, but when you help someone learn, you must get involved with the whole person. Teachers exist to serve the students by providing the tools that would help them learn. In the same vein, McGuire (2015) states that a little bit of personal connection with students helps in the learning process. According to her, when teachers encourage students to visit them during their office hours and teachers take time to know the names of students, especially in a small class, it helps students learn as opposed to treating them anonymous persons. As part of the strategy in helping students learn, teachers can empower them by helping them close the gap between their current behavior and the effective, productive behavior that will result in the grade they want. This improvement in learning for students may involve metacognition.

Metacognition was introduced by Flavell in the early 1970s based on the term "meta memory." (Jadav, 2011) Although metacognition has been a part of educational psychology for the last three decades, this concept helps students become more aware of their ability to be problem solvers, which invariably supports the notion of them actively being involved in the learning process. Metacognition is typically used as a tool to deal with everyday problems such as when to cross the road when there are no oncoming vehicles. It reflects what should be done. As McGuire (2015) puts it, "it is as if you have a big brain outside of your brain looking at what your brain is doing." (p. 235)

Jadav (2011) explained how Metacognition is reflective of the inscription at the oracle of Apollo in Delphi, Greece, that states, "Know thyself." It is also reflective of the words of Socrates's rebuttal when he was found guilty of heresy when he stated, "The life which is unexamined is not worth living." (p. 16)

Metacognition heralds the importance of self-reflection and is a form of observation of an individual of his own conscious action. Having self-awareness, which places metacognition at the pinnacle of personal growth, may support student learning.

Understanding that students come into the classroom with some level of learning based on their culture, race, or societal socialization, it is the teachers' role to assist students in making sense of their prior experience and the environment in which they are learning. The teacher must structure and assist the students by being interactive in making sense of the mental framework in which students come into the classroom with. Teachers can help student learning by igniting students' reflection and interaction skills. Students teaching students is a powerful method of building learning and driving creativity and innovation. Because reflection creates creativity, when students learn to be creative they become better at the learning process.

WHY STUDENTS DO NOT LEARN

Missing Classes

According to Tinto's (2012) persistence theory, students who learn are more likely to want to remain in college in order to continue learning. Learning is a complex phase. The solution for students not learning is non-exhaustive here. However, many students prevent their learning by engaging in behavior that promotes their failures and inhibits learning; one such behavior is missing classes. Sometimes, the attitude of missing classes has several issues, or it is a direct result of their low confidence in their ability to be successful. In missing classes, students exclude themselves from the learning process. While most institutions enforce the responsibility of the teachers to contact absent students, others do not; in the cases of missed classes, students are not able to engage themselves in the complete learning process without difficulties. Most students that miss classes would often ask, "Did I miss anything?" Wayman (1993) created a poem on this subject after experiencing almost the same problem that raises the question from students missing classes.

Did I Miss Anything?
Tom Wayman

Nothing. When we realized you weren't here
we sat with our hands folded on our desks
in silence, for the full two hours
Everything. I gave an exam worth
40 percent of the grade for this term
and assigned some reading due today
on which I'm about to hand out a quiz
worth 50 percent
Nothing. None of the content of this course
has value or meaning
Take as many days off as you like:
any activities we undertake as a class
I assure you will not matter either to you or me
and are without purpose

Everything. A few minutes after we began last time
a shaft of light suddenly descended and an angel
or other heavenly being appeared
and revealed to us what each
woman or man must do
to attain divine wisdom in this life and
the hereafter
This is the last time the class will meet
before we disperse to bring the good
news to all people on earth.
Nothing. When you are not present
how could something significant occur?
Everything. Contained in this classroom
Is a microcosm of human experience?
Assembled for you to query and
examine and ponder
This is not the only place such an
opportunity has been gathered
But it was one place
And you weren't here

Contacting students is one of the solutions to help prevent them from missing classes. Teachers' responsibility in contacting students plays an effective role. Central Oregon Community College in

Bend reported an improved and increased freshman to sophomore year retention when teachers contacted students in the first week that they missed classes. There was a 222 percent retention after faculty made the decision to contact absent students (Weber, 1985).

Passive Educational Institutional Behavior

In this context on passive educational institutional behavior, passive means allowing or permitting what happens in an institution without resistance. It is a yielding perspective where an institution accepts, ignores, or observes trait without responding. Behavior, on the other hand, has been viewed as an observable act, like the singing of a song where the listener observes the singer and listens to the music. To others, behavior refers only to an overt act. Others use behavior to describe and emphasize the active nature of the learner. However, when the institution of learning is passive over teachers' instructional attitude or lack of training, it affects and inhibits the students learning process.

Ornstein, Pajak, and Ornstein (2015) noted that institutional and educational goals are defined as learning to be acquired, support goals as services to be rendered, and management goals as functions of management. When educational institutions are passive over the management of those goals, which are supposed to be executed by teachers, it impacts negatively on student learning. According to the traditional philosophy of teaching, a teacher is an authority on the subject matter. Teachers plan activities, supply knowledge, talk, and dominate lesson plans. Contemporary methods view a teacher as a guide for inquiry and a change agent. However, when institutions are passive over teachers who are not connected to what is expected of them, it hurts students' ability to learn.

Teachers show of love and concern to the students should be the cardinal perspective of every learning institution. This important aspect of teaching should be evaluated if it is truly important to institutions. When institutions are passive about teaching, they cannot access teacher's motivation. Teaching should be committed to a higher purpose, a humanistic moral purpose that is designed beyond academic grades. It also involves social and personal responsibility. However, when the institution is passive about the issue of instructors' outcomes, care, concern, and commitment to students, the institution indirectly, or in some cases, directly promotes a culture that hinders learning.

Students need to know the institution cares for them through the teachers. For example, a teacher at Purdue University in West Lafayette, Indiana, developed the method of expressing his concerns for his students by standing at the door to greet the students and in turn, learn their names and link their names to the faces by learning a few things about the students. The behavior of care when modeled to students enhances the learning process because most students love to learn from people that care about them, especially people they admire.

In addition, a distinguished professor emeritus models another method of care to the students in a different way. Goodchild, (1996) in his study said that the educational administration at the University of Texas at Austin noted that Colvert, many years ago kept up-to-date records of every student he ever had in his doctoral program. According to Goodchild, Colvert knew where they were and what they were doing. While this level of care may be rare and unheard of outside the teaching profession, institutions that are actively promoting such behavior enhances the learning process of students in the care culture they highlight.

In the process of modeling good behavior to students, a positive classroom where the teacher models good mannerisms impact the student's ability to learn. In a good modeling classroom situation, the students believe the instructor is in charge as opposed to a class with a teacher who has a clenching or tweaking mannerism that is destructive to students. This mannerism is also applicable to institutional lack of concerns to teachers that turn students' grades in late.

In modeling good behavior, students have shown that instructors are often not regarded for their listening skills. Studies show that instructors are among the poorest listeners. A good listener concentrates on listening and not spending time listening for their next comments. Good listening entails that students are getting through to teachers in the most appropriate way. If instructors do not read a writing assignment, then they should not be made. Appropriate comment through the text of students' written assignment suggests to students a level of instructor care and listening ability.

Modeling respectful behavior also entails instructors showing respect for their colleagues.

Taking time to excitedly introduce students to their colleagues and not speaking ill of a colleague with students is an excellent part of modeling a culture of respect that institutions should be actively aware of. While being energetic and creating some opportunity for laughter in a classroom is therapeutic, making jest of the institution, colleagues, and students creates tension in a class, which hinders the learning process for students. In a classroom where students are subjected to humiliating and embarrassing processes, they find learning difficult. It is important to note that humiliating processes are not only harmful but could also be positive punishment. For example, when a student is singled out it may not be received well as a positive compliment to others; such an act may be construed as embarrassing.

Students have a right and must feel that those who are essential to their goals believe in them, which means that the goal of the instructor goes beyond teaching. Instead, they should ensure that students learn, as explained by Crim and Vigna. (1983)

Neuman and Finaly-Neuman's (1989) study of junior and senior persistence at a Northeastern University reveals what they referred to as "Quality of Learning experiences." Persistence to learn is linked to students' perceptions of the quality of their learning environment and their interaction with faculty about learning issues. In the study, student learning increases based on their perception of the learning environment, which in most situations is dependent on the institution and the culture the institution promotes.

According to Payne's (2019) work on poverty, she mentioned how a study from the 2004 National Commission on Teaching and America's Future (NCTAF) shows that high poverty schools are more likely than low poverty schools to have many unlicensed teachers in subjects they teach, limited technology access, and insufficient materials. While some schools in high poverty areas implement less rigorous curriculum with fewer experienced teachers, the study concludes that the most disadvantaged children attend schools that do not have basic facilities and conditions conducive to providing them with quality education and as such, hinders students learning.

Learning While Stressed

Learning and memory are essential components of mental functioning. Although separate, they are considered an interrelated process. When a student can retrieve information from their memory storage, learning is assumed to have occurred. Alternatively, if a student cannot remember, it is assumed that learning has not adequately taken place.

In a study conducted by researchers from Rosalind Franklin University of Medicine and Science, researchers discovered that a single socially stressed event could kill new neurons in the brain hippocampus. It is important to note that the hippocampus is one of the regions of the brain that is heavily associated with memory, emotion, and learning. The hippocampus is also one of the regions of the two areas of the brain where neurogenesis, or the formation of new brain cells, occurs throughout life. When a stressful event affects the part of the brain, which is the seat of learning, learning is negatively impacted. There is a growing body of evidence that shows the impact of stress on learning based on an experiment in testing the effect of stress on animals. A research team placed young rats in a cage with two older rats for twenty minutes. The young rats were then subjected to aggression from the more mature rats in the cage. Later, the researcher examined the young rats and found that they had a high cortisol level, six times higher than rats who had not experienced a stressful social encounter.

Another study found that the hippocampus shrank in rats who were exposed to chronic stress. The hippocampus is integral to forming memories. It has been debated before whether post-traumatic stress disorder (PTSD) can shrink the hippocampus, or people with naturally smaller hippocampus are just more prone to PTSD. This study could point to the fact that stress being a factor affects the brain.

The most recent work of Rosenkranz (2019) on stress highlights the study of neurophysiology of emotions and memory. The work further expanded how the amygdala, which is a process (or protrusion) of the brain, mediates and influences emotions and how it affects change during learning. The conclusion of the study on stress shows that stress is a precipitating factor in depression and anxiety disorders. Patients with these disorders often show amygdala abnormalities. The basolateral amygdala (BLA) is integral in mood and emotion and is sensitive to stress changing the brain. In the process of a teacher teaching, even with the best method, the student may not be learning because of the processes.

Mindfulness has been used as one solution for the stress that has inhibited student learning. Stress is not *always* a bad thing, because in some cases it protects us from danger; however, in most learning cases, it impacts negatively on learning depending on the type of stress. Researchers are now learning how stressors can physically alter our brains, which in turn, may impact how we learn, form memories, and even make decisions. Mindfulness is the psychological process of purposely bringing one's attention to experiences occurring in the present moment without judgment.

Mindfulness has long been practiced in Eastern spiritual traditions for personal improvement. Educators and educational institutions have recently begun to explore its usefulness in schools; over the last thirty years, this practice has been thoroughly researched and successfully implemented in hospitals, businesses, education, and the military. Mindfulness training can be valuable in helping students be more successful learners and more connected members of an educational community. To determine if mindfulness instruction should be incorporated into the curriculum at all levels of formal education in order to help students be more successful in their academic pursuits, a thorough review of research was conducted using primary and secondary sources of the possible applications and results of mindfulness in education. In mindfulness education, one must consider stress.

It was helpful in some specific ways, minimizing the impact of bullying, helping students with learning disabilities, benefiting students who are training in careers with high emotion and stress, and coaching. Based on the results, students who have mindfulness incorporated in their curriculum could potentially reap benefits academically and personally. In Figure 1 below, Risky Coping is not retaining information.

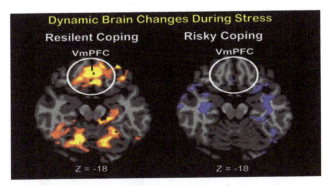

Figure 1. Dynamic brain changes during stress.
Note. Designed by Bill Hathaway from Yale University on the Brain (with permission from the designer).

As it relates to stress caused by economic reasons on learning, Payne (2019) shows in research that was carried out at the University of California, Berkeley, in which the researcher compared low-income in nine-year- and ten-year-old brains with wealthy brains of children of the same age using an EEG. The lead researcher, Mark Kishiyama's statement was eye-opening as it concluded that the brain of children from poverty showed a pattern that is seen in patients who suffered from strokes, where lesions were found in their prefrontal cortex. The research suggests that in these children the prefrontal function is reduced or disrupted in some way. The author concluded that while such deficiency is reversible through intensive intervention such as focused learning and other methods, it is important to note that student learning is negatively impacted by such economic experience.

Hindrances of Technology on Learning

While this topic may not receive a good review given our craving towards the usage of modern technology and our current anticipation for what is next, understandably, technology plays a vital role in the student learning process and plays another inhibitive role in learning, which will be explained after considering the positive roles.

It is arguably true that technology integration in schools is a key to unlocking new educational experiences and re-imagining of pedagogical approaches to teaching and learning. The view exists that meaningful tech integration goes much further than merely using technology; it fuses instructional content with digital tools to reshape the framework of teaching and learning. Tech integration is a pedagogical change in education that supplants traditional teaching methods, changes the student-teacher dynamic, and delivers learning in new and better ways.

With so much seemingly riding on the quality and efficacy of this effort, we ask, "*What constitutes meaningful tech integration?*"

While the need for technology exists, it is essential to note that our society has been engulfed by a crisis of concentration that has hit higher education particularly hard. According to Newport (2019), an associate professor of computer science at Georgetown University, "Our time and attention have gradually shifted from the specialized intellectual tasks that directly produce value to busywork, such as managing our inboxes and tackling nonessential administrative obligations." With the management of nonessential tasks in higher education, the concentration that ought to be given to student learning has been left out.

The academic institution of learning, which is supposed to be considered the beacon of concentration in an age of technology distractions, has negatively impacted learning. While technology is designed to improve student learning, it has been found to have taken a different position. Newport (2019) suggests that higher education can lead the way in turning back the tide of electronic chatter that threatens to overwhelm us by embracing deep concentration on learning. Three solutions to the problem of technology hindering learning should be 1) conceptualizing undisruptive tech integration, 2) assessing approaches for developing impactful, tech-driven learning experiences, and 3) equipping educators with strategies to integrate technology meaningfully, effectively, and disruptively only for the purpose that there is a measurable outcome that it improves learning.

REFERENCES

Baker, R. 2016. "The effect of structured transfer pathways in community colleges." *Educational Evaluation and Policy Analysis*. doi:10.3102/0162373737716651491

Bouton, M. E. 2007. *Learning and behavior: A contemporary synthesis*. Sinauer Associates.

Boyer, E. L. 1997. *Ernest L. Boyer: Selected speeches, 1979–1995*. San Francisco, CA: Jossey-Bass Inc., Publishers.

Crim, J.W., and Vigna, S.R. 1983. "Brain, gut, and skin peptide hormones in lower vertebrates." *American Zoologist*, *23*(3), 621–638.

Ebbinghaus, H. 1885. *Über das gedächtnis: Uuntersuchungen zur experimentellen psychologie*. Duncker & Humblot.

Ebbinghaus, K.D. 1962. "Experience in the treatment of urinary tract infections with a plant antibiotic (Tromacaps). *Die Medizinische Welt*, *23*, 1327–1329.

Fosnot, C.T. 1989. "Enquiring teachers." *Enquiring Learners: A Constructivist Approach for Teaching, New York: Teachers College, Columbia University.*

Gabriel, K.F. 2008. *Teaching unprepared students.* Sterling, VA: Stylus.

Gallimore, R., and Tharp, R. G. 1990. "Teaching mind and society: A theory of education and schooling." *Vygotsky and Education: Instructional Implications and Applications of Sociohistorical Psychology*, 175–205.

Goodchild, L. F. 1996. "G. Stanley Hall and the study of higher education." *Review of Higher Education, 20(1)*69–99.

Hillman, N. 2014. "College on Credit: A multilevel analysis of student loan default." *The Review of Higher Education*, *37, 169–195.*

Hufstedler, S. M. 1979. "Shirley M. Hufstedler papers", 1979–1981. Manuscript Division, Library of Congress, Washington, DC Library of Congress.

Jadav, V.B.G. 2011. "Construction and standardization of a metacognition inventory for the students of secondary schools and study of metacognition in context of some variables University (India)." ProQuest Dissertations Publishing, 2011. 3735090.

McGuire, S.Y. 2015. *Teach students how to learn: Strategies you can incorporate into any course to improve student metacognition, study skills, and motivation.* Sterling, Virginia: Stylus Publisher.

Neumann, Y., and Finaly-Neumann, E. 1989. "Predicting juniors' and seniors' persistence and attrition: A quality of learning experience approach." *The Journal of Experimental Education, 57*(2), 129–140.

Newport, C. 2019. *Digital minimalism: Choosing a focused life in a noisy world.* Penguin.

O'Dowd, R. 2015. "The competences of the telecollaborative teacher." *The Language Learning Journal, 43*(2), 194–207.

Ornstein, A.O., Pajak, E.G., and Ornstein, S.B. 2015. *Contemporary issues in curriculum,* (6th Edition), Pearson.

Payne, R. K. 2019. *A framework for understanding poverty: A cognitive approach,* (6th Edition) Highland, TX. Aha process.

Rosenkranz, J. 2019. *Disruptive effects of repeated stress on basolateral amygdala neurons and fear behav-*

ior across the estrous cycle in rats. National Center for Biotechnology Information, U. S. National Library of Medicine. Retrieved from https://www.ncbi.nlm.nih.gov/pubmed/31444385

Schwartz, B., Wasserman, E., and Robbins, S. 2002. *Psychology of learning and behaviour* (ed.). London: Norton & Company.

Thorndike, E.L. 1911. *Individuality.* Boston, MA: Houghton, Mifflin.

Tinto, V. 2012. *Completing college: Rethinking institutional action.* Chicago, Il: University of Chicago Press.

Vygotsky, L.S. 1962. "Thought and Language, edited and translated by E. Hanfmann and G. Vakar." Cambridge, MA: MIT Press. doi, 10, 11193-000.

Wayman, T. 1993. *Did I miss anything? Selected poems, 1973–1993.* Pender Harbour, CA: Harbour Publishing Company.

Weber, J. 1985. "Assessment and placement: A review of the research." *Community College Review*, *13*(3), 21–32.

Wilkinson, B. 2010. *Almost every answer for practically any teacher: The seven laws of the learner series.* Atlanta, GA: Multnomah Publishers.

ABOUT THE AUTHOR

Evans Igho Akpo is a full-time faculty member at South Texas College in McAllen, Texas, where he teaches Government and provides support to student's leadership. Before joining South Texas College, he served as an Adjunct Assistant Professor at Cosumnes River College in Sacramento, California, and as an Employment Coordinator with the State of California in San Jose, California.

His studies and career experiences from British American College, now Regent's University, London, United Kingdom, to Webster University in St. Louis, Missouri prepared him for a focused, project-based learning. Evans began his career as a Graduate Writing Coach at Webster University and served as an instructional coach at Cosumnes River College where he led a mentoring graduate program.

He holds a bachelor's and master's degrees in International Relations, and his doctoral studies focused on student success. While completing his doctoral internship at Houston Community College, Coleman College for Health Sciences in Houston, he assisted in areas of supporting students' success with early alerts. His area of specialty is analyzing the dynamics and factors likely to help improve the success rate of targeted groups of students.

As an educational leader and teacher, Evans believes if students are provided with the intended resources and support system, most students will unleash their genius as they persist, learn, succeed, and thrive throughout college. He is the author of *Are the Students Learning?*

CPSIA information can be obtained
at www.ICGtesting.com
Printed in the USA
LVHW021055020721
691719LV00008B/64